Ephesians
Bible Study

Righteously Redeemed

Aromi M. Knox

Ephesians Bible Study: Righteously Redeemed. Copyright © by Aromi Knox.

All rights reserved. Printed in the United States of America.

No part of this book may be used or reproduced in any manner whatsoever without written permission except in the case of brief quotations embodied in critical articles and reviews.

For information, address DW Creative Publishers, 4261 E. University Dr. #30-355; Prosper, TX 75078.

DW Creative Publishers books may be purchased for business, educational, religious, or sales promotional use. For information, please email connect@dwcreativepublishers.com.

To connect with the author, Aromi Knox or Righteously Redeemed, visit www.righteouslyredeemed.org.

FIRST EDITION
Cover design by: DW Creative Publishers
Interior design by: DW Creative Publishers
Editing by: DW Creative Publishers

ISBN 978-1-952605-20-8

Table Of Contents

Introduction

Chapter One	1
Chapter Two	21
Chapter Three	44
Chapter Four	65
Chapter Five	85
Chapter Six	102
Leaders Guide	126

Introduction

Let me start by saying nothing will ever fully satisfy or replace the importance and impact of reading the Bible. The Word of God is living and produces so much peace, encouragement, and guidance. As you begin this Bible study, please utilize it as a guide. Never replace actually reading the entire chapter. The book of Ephesians is powerful and will directly impact the way you live your life as a Christ follower.

Throughout this study, you will have areas to color while reflecting over God's Word. Each day has a song listed for you to listen to and worship throughout the day to keep your heart and thoughts fixed on the Lord. Taking time to settle your mind and pace of life allows the Holy Spirit to speak to you without the worldly distractions.

I encourage you to read scripture on your own first, then share and discuss with your friends. Reading the Bible in your own quiet time allows for the Holy Spirit to move and speak to you. Another suggestion is to read the chapters in different Bible versions. It is helpful to hear the Word of God through different translations as one may resonate with you differently over another.

Chapter One

Background of the Writing of Ephesians: The apostle Paul wrote this book to the church of Ephesus while he was in prison.

Note to leader: Begin each chapter by reflecting on what the group is thankful for. Ask if there are any prayer requests. These may be shared aloud or silently to pray.

What are you thankful for?

_____
_____
_____

Prayer requests

_____
_____
_____

For he chose us

Day One

Ephesians 1:4-5, NIV

For he chose us in him before the creation of the world to be holy and blameless in his sight. In love he predestined us for adoption to sonship through Jesus Christ, in accordance with his pleasure and will.

This question came from Dr. Tony Evans and is very thought provoking.

How should knowing you were handpicked by God, by changing the way you view yourself?

_____
_____
_____
_____

The definition of adopted/adoption is the action or fact of choosing to take up, follow, or use something. There is no human difference between an adopted child and one who is born into the biological family.

Why do you think people adopt?

___

How does the concept of adoption relate to why God would have Paul choose the word "adopted" to describe our acceptance into the family of Christ?

___

Song: Champion by Bethel Music & Dante Bowe

In him we have redemption through his blood, the forgiveness of sins, in accordance with the riches of God's grace.

Day Two

Ephesians 1:7, NIV

In him we have redemption through his blood, the forgiveness of sins, in accordance with the riches of God's grace.

What do you consider sin?

Make a list:

_____   _____
_____   _____
_____   _____
_____   _____
_____   _____

Redemption

This question also stemmed from Dr. Tony Evans.

How should you live knowing that Jesus paid such an expensive price to redeem you?

_____
_____
_____
_____
_____

Redemption: to buy or purchase something. We were slaves to sin, but Christ redeemed us. The price was the Son of God, Christ Jesus, pure and blameless.

Song: For.ev.er.more by Ryan Brockington

Day Three

1 Peter 1:18-19, NIV

For you know that it was not with perishable things such as silver or gold that you were redeemed from the empty way of life handed down to you from your ancestors, but with the precious blood of Christ, a lamb without blemish or defect.

When we think about expensive things, what comes to mind? What is the most expensive thing you own?

_____
_____
_____
_____

Now think about that item(s) and imagine it being gone forever?

The greatest thing about our Lord and Savior is He will never leave us. His death on the cross was the greatest cost and it has been given to us freely. FREE.

His love: free.
His forgiveness: free.
His blessings: free.
His mercy: free.

Nothing in this world will ever be as expensive as His sacrifice for us so that we can live in eternity with Him.

His love: free.
His forgiveness: free.
His blessings: free.
His mercy: free.

Many people are afraid to lose things, possessions, gifts, jobs, friends, family, and even their own life, but know that as children of God, **we do not lose**. We will always win because our prize is eternal. There is a promise for a life full of peace, no tears, no pain, and it will be in heaven.

"He will wipe every tear from their eyes, and there will be no more death or sorrow or crying or pain. All these things are gone forever" (Revelation 21:4, NLT).

Song: Simple by Elevation Rhythm featuring Joe L. Barnes

In him we were also chosen

Day Four

Ephesians 1:11, NIV
In him we were also chosen, having been predestined according to the plan of him who works out everything in conformity with the purpose of his will.

How have you felt when a group, organization, employer, or person you wanted to be chosen by did not choose you?

_____
_____
_____

The feeling of rejection is hard. It can be confusing and even make you question your value and worth. But this is not true. You have been chosen and you are wanted by God. Your Father in Heaven picks you and I every single day. He wants to be close with us and pour out His love, protection, and grace every minute of every hour of every day. You are His first pick.

Song: Praise Before My Breakthrough by Bryan & Katie Torwalt

Day Five

Ephesians 1:15-16, NIV

For this reason, ever since I heard about your faith in the Lord Jesus and your love for all God's people, I have not stopped giving thanks for you, remembering you in my prayers.

Who do you need to be praying for? Maybe it is someone who is new to the faith or maybe someone who is struggling with their faith. Take a couple minutes and write down anyone that comes to your mind. If you are having trouble, ask the Lord to help you.

_____
_____
_____
_____
_____

Hope

Ephesians 1:18-21, NIV
I pray that the eyes of your heart may be enlightened in order that you may know the hope to which he has called you, the riches of his glorious inheritance in his holy people, and his incomparably great power for us who believe. That power is the same as the mighty strength he exerted when he raised Christ from the dead and seated him at his right hand in the heavenly realms, far above all rule and authority, power and dominion, and every name that is invoked, not only in the present age but also in the one to come.

This is powerful. HOPE. God gives HOPE. If you are lacking hope, it is not because of God. He gives hope. Have you felt depressed, not excited or looking forward to the future? That feeling is from the enemy, and you CANNOT let him win over your emotions or thoughts.

Your Father is mighty and all-powerful. He has an inheritance for you. Heaven is coming. But until then, He needs you here to share, spread, and shine for Him in your life. He has plans for you. **Jeremiah 29:11 states,** "'For I know the plans I have for you,' declares the Lord, 'plans to prosper you and not to harm you, plans to give you hope and a future.'" God knows the plans because He made them. There is HOPE for you and His power can and will work through you if you accept it and allow it.

What are you hoping for in your life?

Song: Everlasting God by William Murphy

Chapter Reflection

Chapter Two

Note to leader: Begin each chapter by reflecting on what the group is thankful for. Ask if there are any prayer requests. These may be shared aloud or silently to pray.

What are you thankful for?

_____
_____
_____

Prayer requests

_____
_____
_____
_____
_____
_____
_____
_____
_____
_____
_____
_____

This is the confidence we have in approaching God: that if we ask anything according to his will, he hears us.

Day One

1 John 5:14, NIV

This is the confidence we have in approaching God: that if we ask anything according to his will, he hears us.

Ephesians 2:1-2, NIV

As for you, you were dead in your transgressions and sins, in which you used to live when you followed the ways of this world and of the ruler of the kingdom of the air, the spirit who is now at work in those who are disobedient.

What is one thing you used to do, but have stopped doing?

_____
_____
_____
_____
_____

What is one thing you want to stop doing, but have not stopped doing yet?

_____
_____
_____
_____

Pray aloud with your group or silently.

Ask God to help you in this area. Tell Him you need His help to overcome this struggle and attachment to the world and no longer want to feed your fleshly desires.

Transformation does not come overnight or in a single day. Many of our habits have been built over years of living and being in this world. As we recognize our acceptance and freedom in Christ Jesus, our lives begin to change, including the way we think and act.

Song: Ask by Love & The Outcome

Jesus is our redemption

Day Two

Ephesians 2:4-5, NIV
But because of his great love for us, God, who is rich in mercy, made us alive with Christ even when we were dead in transgressions—it is by grace you have been saved.

We used to live in sin, not even knowing what we did was sinful, but once we entered the Body of Christ and began to learn His character and Word, our passions and desires started to change. The best and sweetest part of this is God's mercy and grace that covers us and blesses us while forgiving us and not giving us the punishment of death that we deserve. Jesus is our redemption.

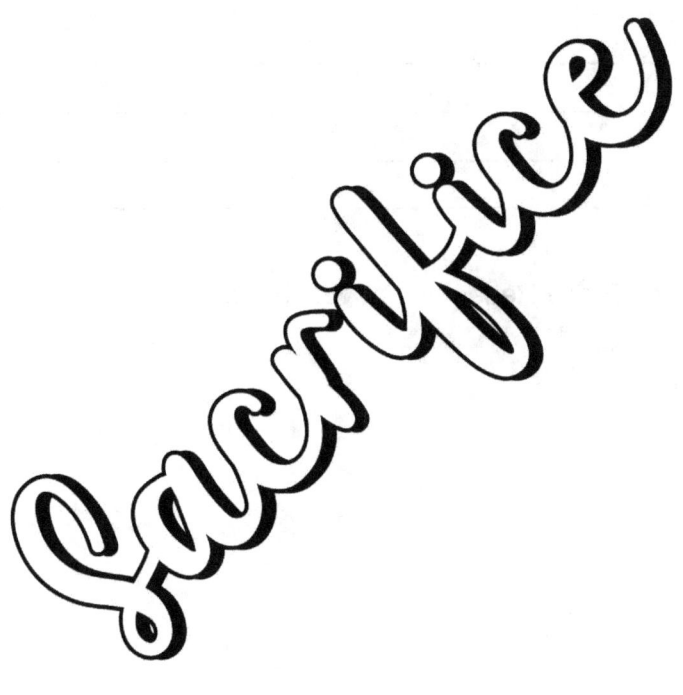

1 John 4:10, NIV

This is real love—not that we loved God, but that he loved us and sent his Son as a sacrifice to take away our sins.

What does sacrifice mean to you?

_____
_____
_____
_____
_____
_____

Song: Grace Redeemed by Fresh Start Worship

Faith

Day Three

Ephesians 2:8-9, NIV

For it is by grace you have been saved, through faith—and this is not from yourselves, it is the gift of God—not by works, so that no one can boast.

Write down how you would describe faith to someone.

_____
_____
_____
_____

How do you show your faith in action?

_____
_____
_____
_____

What is something you are really good at, and would you be willing to help someone grow in that area? Why or why not?

_____
_____
_____

Salvation is a gift

I love this question because it humbles us, but also allows for recognition to be given. The thing(s) we are really good at is not by our own ability. God gave us those gifts, talent, drive, and ability. It is Him working through us. When we try to take credit for our good deeds or work, we are discrediting God, our Creator.

It is the same with our salvation. Salvation is a gift freely given by God through His love, grace, and goodness. The repetition and remembrance is needed so we do not forget WHO has blessed us with our freedom and abilities. It is God and God alone. Give credit where credit is deserved.

Song: Faithful by Sarah Reeves

Day Four

Ephesians 2:10, NLT
For we are God's masterpiece. He has created us anew in Christ Jesus, so we can do the good things he planned for us long ago.

Masterpiece: a work of outstanding artistry, skill, or workmanship. You.

It can be hard to believe or even view yourself as a masterpiece – someone who is defined as outstanding. Do you view yourself as outstanding? God does. He views you as perfect, redeemed, and good. In fact, the Bible tells us, every good and perfect gift comes from the Lord. You came from Him; He is your Creator.

He is your Creator

List five good things about yourself.

1.
2.
3.
4.
5.

Song: Royalty by Tasha Cobbs

Day Five

Before Jesus Christ, the Jews believed and some still believe they are the chosen ones, meaning the only ones going to heaven and currently waiting for their Savior, who they do not believe is Jesus Christ. If you are not a Jew, then you are considered a Gentile. I am a Gentile and you are a Gentile. Jesus Christ, however, paved the way for both Jews and Gentiles to come to Him and receive eternal life and a home in Heaven. No more separation. No more exclusion.

You have Been Accepted

Make a list of different people groups. For example, Blacks and Whites.

_____
_____
_____
_____

So, you see, it does not matter your gender, race, color, origin, political background, career, economic status, bank account, or family history. YOU HAVE BEEN ACCEPTED through the death and resurrection of Jesus Christ. He is the forgiveness of our sins. He is our saving Grace. He is our ride or die.

Ephesians 2:13-16, NIV
But now in Christ Jesus you who once were far away have been brought near by the blood of Christ. For he himself is our peace, who has made the two groups one and has destroyed the barrier, the dividing wall of hostility, by setting aside in his flesh the law with its commands and regulations. His purpose was to create in himself one new humanity out of the two, thus making peace, and in one body to reconcile both of them to God through the cross, by which he put to death their hostility.

Jesus came so there may be peace between and within

His creation, His children who have accepted Him and welcomed Him into their lives and hearts and directs their actions.

for he himself is our peace

Ephesians 2:21-22, NIV

In him the whole building is joined together and rises to become a holy temple in the Lord And in him you too are being built together to become a dwelling in which God lives by his Spirit.

How can you continue to grow God's Kingdom and reflect His peace towards others?

_____
_____
_____
_____

Song: You are Holy (Prince of Peace) by Michael W. Smith

Chapter Reflection

Chapter Three

Note to leader: Begin each chapter by reflecting on what the group is thankful for. Ask if there are any prayer requests. These may be shared aloud or silently to pray.

What are you thankful for?

_____
_____
_____

Prayer requests

_____
_____
_____

Prisoner for Christ

Day One

Ephesians 3:1, NIV

For this reason I, Paul, the prisoner of Christ Jesus for the sake of you Gentiles—

What does it mean to be a prisoner for Christ?

_____
_____
_____
_____
_____

Would you rather be a slave to your sins or to Jesus? When we think about a slave or a prisoner, we think about being owned by someone else and under their control. Who is in control of your life? Your flesh or the Spirit? The enemy or Christ? Who are you living your life for – the world or eternity in Heaven?

Who is in control of your life?

What have you felt a prisoner to?
_____
_____
_____
_____
_____
_____

Song: No Longer Slaves by Bethel Music, Jonathan David, & Melissa Helser

grace

Day Two

Romans 6:11-19, NIV

For we know that our old self was crucified with him so that the body ruled by sin might be done away with, that we should no longer be slaves to sin—because anyone who has died has been set free from sin.

In the same way, count yourselves dead to sin but alive to God in Christ Jesus.   Therefore do not let sin reign in your mortal body so that you obey its evil desires. Do not offer any part of yourself to sin as an instrument of wickedness, but rather offer yourselves to God as those who have been brought from death to life; and offer every part of yourself to him as an instrument of righteousness. For sin shall no longer be your master because you are not under the law, but under grace.

Don't you know that when you offer yourselves to someone as obedient slaves, you are slaves of the one you obey—whether you are slaves to sin, which leads to death, or to obedience, which leads to righteousness?

You have been set free from sin and have become slaves to righteousness. I am using an example from everyday life because of your human limitations. Just as you used to offer yourselves as slaves to impurity and to ever-increasing wickedness, so now offer yourselves as slaves to righteousness leading to holiness.

How do these verses empower you to want to change your life?

_____
_____
_____
_____
_____
_____
_____
_____
_____
_____
_____
_____
_____
_____
_____

Holiness

Do you feel empowered and able to make the changes needed in your life to live free from sin and walk boldly in the righteousness of God our Father?

_____
_____
_____

Song: Made New by Lincoln Brewster

Just the desire to believe.

Day Three

Ephesians 3:6, NIV
This mystery is that through the gospel the Gentiles are heirs together with Israel, members together of one body, and sharers together in the promise in Christ Jesus.
What is the Gospel? How would you describe it?

_____
_____
_____
_____
_____

Here is a video you can watch: <u>The Gospel in Four Minutes</u> by Pipeline Generation— "GOSPEL: God Our Sins Paying Everyone Life."

One thing you can consider is your walk with Christ and how sharing the Gospel requires   only faith the size of a mustard seed. Just the desire to believe.

Philippians 3:12-14, NIV
I'm not saying that I have this all together, that I have it made. But I am well on my way, reaching out for Christ, who has so wondrously reached out for me. Friends, don't

get me wrong: By no means do I count myself an expert in all of this, but I've got my eye on the goal, where God is beckoning us onward—to Jesus. I'm off and running, and I'm not turning back.

I know it can be challenging sometimes to share the Word of God due to your past or your level of faith or ability to describe what is in the Bible. However, we are not expected to know, grow and transform at the same time. We all grow at our own pace. There is grace to be given and received in our walk with the Lord. Paul does a great job explaining this and relating to us in this way. He reminds us that he does not even feel like an expert to share, but he does it anyway and we can too!

Song: Gotta Believe by Tasha Cobbs Leonard

In him and through faith in him we may approach God with freedom and confidence.

Day Four

Ephesians 3:12-13, NIV

In him and through faith in him we may approach God with freedom and confidence. I ask you, therefore, not to be discouraged because of my sufferings for you, which are your glory.

There is a major difference between the Old Testament and the New Testament. God did not change, but when he sent Jesus, His death and resurrection changed everything!

We live in a time where we can access and speak to the Lord anytime. Through the Holy Spirit, we can conversate, pray, and receive guidance from Him. We read in Exodus 33 where Moses receives access to the Lord through speaking to Him in a tent and the cloud of God appears.

This story makes me think back to when I was child and every time I heard thunder, I thought, maybe that is God speaking to us.

What does it mean to approach God with freedom and confidence?

_____

_____

Ephesians 3:17-19, NIV

So that Christ may dwell in your hearts through faith. And I pray that you, being rooted and established in love, may have power, together with all the Lord's holy people, to grasp how wide and long and high and deep is the love of Christ, and to know this love that surpasses knowledge—that you may be filled to the measure of all the fullness of God.

His love surpasses all our knowledge. We are not supposed to fully understand it and it is okay if you do not understand it all. We are not supposed to. God's love surpasses our knowledge.

Coming together allows us to experience and understand His power and how wide, long, high, and deep His love and grace is for us. Think of the ocean – it is never-ending, and we will never fully know its depth. This is how much God loves us.

Song: Where Do I Fit In? by Justin Bieber featuring Tori Kelly, Chandler Moore & Judah Smith

Now all glory to God, who is able, through his mighty power at work within us, to accomplish infinitely more than we might ask or think.

Day Five

Ephesians 3:20, NIV
Now to him who is able to do immeasurably more than all we ask or imagine, according to his power that is at work within us,

Ephesians 3:20 NLT
Now all glory to God, who is able, through his mighty power at work within us, to accomplish infinitely more than we might ask or think.

Ephesians 3:20-21, MSG
God can do anything, you know—far more than you could ever imagine or guess or request in your wildest dreams! He does it not by pushing us around but by working within us, his Spirit deeply and gently within us.

Which translation resonates with you the best? Describe why.

_____
_____
_____

I love these verses in all of these translations. How amazing is our God? He does infinitely and immeasurably more than our wildest dreams. This makes me want to jump up and down, twirl around and tell everyone I meet.

When things in our life go far better than we could ever imagine, that is God. You do not have to believe Him for Him to be working in your life. He loves you whether or not you acknowledge Him. He will continue to show up in your life in the hopes that you see Him and His goodness working through you. I believe He does this so that one day people who are far from Him will come to the knowledge and acceptance of who He is.

Scripture tells that one day, "every knee will bow, and every tongue will confess" (Romans 14:11).

Philippians 2:9-11, NIV
Therefore God exalted him to the highest place and gave him the name that is above every name, that at the name of Jesus every knee should bow, in heaven and on earth and under the earth, and every tongue acknowledge that Jesus Christ is Lord, to the glory of God the Father.

Romans 14:11, NIV
It is written: "'As surely as I live,' says the Lord, 'every knee will bow before me; every tongue will acknowledge God.'"
What has God done in your life that has blown you away?

This could be something you had never expected to actually happen or see accomplished?

_____
_____
_____
_____

What are you continuing to believe God for in your life? You have not seen it yet, but you are trusting and waiting on His perfect timing.

_____
_____
_____
_____

Something I know full and well is God will not withhold anything you need. He is Jehovah Jireh, our provider. Rest assured, if you do not have it now, it is because you do not need it or because God is waiting for the right time to give it to you. Once you know this, remind yourself of this often so the enemy will not make you feel as if you are lacking. I promise you that you have all you need. He's got you covered!

Song: Waymaker by Sinach

Chapter Four

Note to leader: Begin each chapter by reflecting on what the group is thankful for. Ask if there are any prayer requests. These may be shared aloud or silently to pray.

What are you thankful for?
_____
_____
_____
_____

Prayer requests
_____
_____
_____
_____

Be completely humble and gentle; be patient, bearing with one another in love.

Day One

You have made it halfway through Ephesians. Don't rush through these next few chapters. Ask the Holy Spirit to speak to you through these verses and watch Him move in your life.

Before reading Scripture, prepare your hearts.

Let's start with this: Is there anyone you are upset with in your life? It could be an individual or a people group you have trouble within your heart or thoughts. Prepare yourself as you are about to be challenged in this regard. Do not dismiss it and do not exclude yourself from it. Once you know better, do better.

Ephesians 4:1-3, NIV
As a prisoner for the Lord, then, I urge you to live a life worthy of the calling you have received. Be completely humble and gentle; be patient, bearing with one another in love. Make every effort to keep the unity of the Spirit through the bond of peace.

Ephesians 4:29-32, NIV
Do not let any unwholesome talk come out of your mouths, but only what is helpful for building others up according to

their needs, that it may benefit those who listen. And do not grieve the Holy Spirit of God, with whom you were sealed for the day of redemption. Get rid of all bitterness, rage and anger, brawling and slander, along with every form of malice. Be kind and compassionate to one another, forgiving each other, just as in Christ God forgave you.

We are going to allow this chapter to release bitterness, rage, anger, and any other feelings that are not of God. Did you know that the enemy can use you? He does not even have to do much. He is the accuser of the brethren. We have to use the Word of God to fight against our fleshly thoughts and feelings towards people who upset us.

Be kind and compassionate to one another, forgiving each other, just as in Christ God forgave you.

Take the next three days and write down any offenses you have been holding on to. Pray for these people or events. Reread these specific verses every day for three days. Do not only read it one time and move on. Ask God to soften your heart and transform your thinking. On our own, we cannot forgive, but through God's love and forgiveness, we can do it.

Do not forget, you are not perfect. You mess up and will have more times in life where you will fall short. We all do, and Scripture tells us about it in **Romans 3:22-25 (NIV).**

This righteousness is given through faith in[h] Jesus Christ to all who believe. There is no difference between Jew and Gentile, for all have sinned and fall short of the glory of God, and all are justified freely by his grace through the redemption that came by Christ Jesus. God presented Christ as a sacrifice of atonement, through the shedding of his blood—to be received by faith. He did this to demonstrate his righteousness, because in his forbearance he had left the sins committed beforehand unpunished.

As you journal over the next two days, here are some questions to guide you. Answer them honestly. Be true to yourself because God already knows how you feel.

Note: If you feel led to share what you write over the next two days, feel free to do so with the group.

Song: Have it All by Fresh Start Worship

Day Two

When do you feel you lose your gentleness or patience?

_____
_____
_____
_____

What are some reasons you think you lose your gentleness or patience?

_____
_____
_____
_____
_____
_____
_____
_____
_____
_____

Song: The Love Inside by Laura Hackett Park

Day Three

When feeling like you are about to become impatient, what do you do to calm down or redirect your thoughts?

_____
_____
_____
_____
_____
_____
_____
_____
_____
_____
_____
_____
_____
_____
_____
_____
_____
_____

One verse that may help before you begin to respond with harsh or abrasive words is Proverbs 16:24 (NLT): *Kind* words are like honey—sweet to the soul and healthy for the body. Ask the Holy Spirit to speak through you and allow your words to be sweet like honey.

Song: Reckless Love by Cory Asbury

one Lord,
one faith,
one baptism,
one God

Day Four

Ephesians 4:5-6, NIV
There is one Lord, one faith, one baptism, one God and Father of all, who is over all, in all, and living through all.

Have you been water baptized?

If not, I encourage you to ask your local church about baptism and get signed up.

Baptism is not a requirement of faith, but it is your outward expression of your inward decision. This is very similar to why people have wedding ceremonies where many people gather as witnesses. This makes your commitment public and known, and the people who witness it can help you remain accountable for your decision. Let all the world know your love and dedication to your great Creator.

Ephesians 4:11-12, NLT

Now these are the gifts Christ gave to the church: the apostles, the prophets, the evangelists, and the pastors and teachers. Their responsibility is to equip God's people to do his work and build up the church, the body of Christ.

Have you thought about your gifts? What are they?

_____
_____
_____
_____
_____
_____

Do you believe God has given you gifts? Well, He has. You can take a spiritual gifts assessment to determine what your spiritual gifts are if you don't currently know them. I encourage you to take a couple of these assessments to see where you have an overlap. These assessments can be found by conducting a simple search on the internet. You can also read 1 Corinthians 12 about the variety of gifts God gives.

Song: Blessed & Favoured by CSO

We won't be tossed and blown about by every wind of new teaching.

Day Five

Ephesians 4:14-15, NIV
Then we will no longer be immature like children. We won't be tossed and blown about by every wind of new teaching. We will not be influenced when people try to trick us with lies so clever they sound like the truth. Instead, we will speak the truth in love, growing in every way more and more like Christ, who is the head of his body, the church.

This verse reminds us, the body of Christ, that we have to be aware of the teaching that we listen to. Not everyone who is preaching the Word of God is giving you truth. If you hear that you have to work for your faith or you have to be a good person to get into Heaven, this is not the truth.

There are many false prophets trying to convince people of a works-based faith and some even purport that giving money is a means to get closer to God. For example, some will state that if you give a certain amount of money, you will receive healing or some other blessing as a result. As a Christian, you give to God out of your obedience and love for His kingdom, not to get anything in return. It is an offering, and you are simply giving back what He gave to you to begin with, with the expectation that your giving will grow His Kingdom and benefit others as they journey through life.

What are some lies you may have been told about the Gospel?

Put on your new nature, created to be like God-truly righteous and holy.

Ephesians 4:19-24, NLT

They have no sense of shame. They live for lustful pleasure and eagerly practice every kind of impurity. But that isn't what you learned about Christ. Since you have heard about Jesus and have learned the truth that comes from him, throw off your old sinful nature and your former way of life, which is corrupted by lust and deception. Instead, let the Spirit renew your thoughts and attitudes. Put on your new nature, created to be like God—truly righteous and holy.

What is one thing you can ask a trusted friend to pray with you to overcome?

_____
_____
_____
_____

We are encouraged and told to throw off our sinful nature or our old way of life. When we enter into a safe community, which can be the company of one person or several people, they can walk with you and help keep you accountable.

_____
_____
_____
_____

Ephesians 4:25, NIV

So stop telling lies. Let us tell our neighbors the truth, for we are all parts of the same body.

Have you told any lies lately? What about lies to yourself about yourself?

_____
_____
_____
_____

Ephesians 4:26-27, NIV

And "don't sin by letting anger control you."[d] Don't let the sun go down while you are still angry, for anger gives a foothold to the devil.

Controlling our anger can be challenging, but we have more control over it than we realize. While it may feel like this is how you have always been and nothing will change, does not mean that it has to be that way. The enemy will use anything to make you feel defeated and push you further away from modeling Christ-like behavior. Do not let him win in this area. Resist the temptation, resist the devil and he will flee from you.

Song: Be Still and Know by David & Nicole Binion

Chapter Five

Note to leader: Begin each chapter by reflecting on what the group is thankful for. Ask if there are any prayer requests. These may be shared aloud or silently to pray.

What are you thankful for?
_____
_____
_____

Prayer requests
_____
_____
_____

Live a life
filled
with love

Day One

Ephesians 5:1-2, NLT

Imitate God, therefore, in everything you do, because you are his dear children. Live a life filled with love, following the example of Christ. He loved us[a] and offered himself as a sacrifice for us, a pleasing aroma to God.

Do you see yourself as a child of God?

Reflect on this question. How is your relationship with your mom and dad? Are you close to each other? Do you listen to them and take their advice? Would you want to imitate their lives?

_____
_____
_____
_____
_____

This next chapter is going to be another challenge. Are you ready?

Imitate Him

If you think about your parents as not being people you would imitate, it can be hard to obey your Heavenly Father. He has expectations and a standard for our lives that protects us from the enemy and from ourselves. As you read, do not give excuses or compare your life to how your friends and family may live their lives. You are reading how God wants you to live – imitate HIM.

Name three things from Ephesians 5:3-5(NLT) that you have done.

Let there be no sexual immorality, impurity, or greed among you. Such sins have no place among God's people. Obscene stories, foolish talk, and coarse jokes—these are not for you. Instead, let there be thankfulness to God. You can be sure that no immoral, impure, or greedy person will inherit the Kingdom of Christ and of God. For a greedy person is an idolater, worshiping the things of this world.

1_____
2_____
3_____

The Bible gives us direction on how to live, but many choose not to follow it fully and instead pick and choose what we want to apply to our lives. I challenge you to break this stigma. Do not follow culture, picking and choosing which parts of the Bible you want to apply to your life.

If you have been living this way, I encourage you to confess, ask for forgiveness, and repent, which means to turn away from this way of living. Remember, according to Romans 8:1, *there is no condemnation for those who are in Christ Jesus.*

If you begin to feel shame, know that it is not the same as conviction. When you love someone, you likely don't want to do things to break their heart. The same goes for God. When you love God, the Person who gave you life and created you fully in His image, you do not want to displease Him. Live to please the Lord and make Him proud.

Activity: Draw a sun and on each ray, write how you want to live. Let Jesus shine through your life.

Song: I'll Give Thanks by Housefires featuring Kirby Kaple

Day Two

Reflect on your drawing from yesterday and the ways you want to live a life that imitates and pleases God.

How did you do today? What are some ways you can begin to identify worldly behaviors and begin living a more Christ-like life? Remember we are in this world, but not of it.

_____
_____
_____
_____
_____
_____
_____
_____
_____
_____
_____
_____
_____
_____
_____
_____

Song: Wildfire by Fuse

God's Purpose

Day Three

Ephesians 5:15-16, TPT

So be very careful how you live, not being like those with no understanding, but live honorably with true wisdom, for we are living in evil times. Take full advantage of every day as you spend your life for his purposes.

What is one thing you did today that pleased the Lord?

_____
_____
_____
_____
_____
_____

What do you think God's purpose is for your life?

_____
_____
_____
_____
_____
_____

How do you intend to spend your life living for God's purpose?

_____
_____
_____
_____
_____
_____

Song: Do Life Big by Jamie Grace

And out of your reverence for Christ be supportive of each other in love.

Day Four

Guide for Marriage

I have always wondered why Paul includes some instructions for marriage in this book. Maybe he knew that in this world, all of the evil could disrupt a godly marriage. Living in drunkenness, lust, greed, and sexual immorality could destroy marriages and Paul wanted to warn us against these consequences. Paul's desire was for his readers to have control over these areas of our lives before entering into marriage because if not, these behaviors can cause major damage to a marriage.

Ephesians 5:21, TPT
And out of your reverence for Christ be supportive of each other in love.

Ephesians 5:21, MSG
Out of respect for Christ, be courteously reverent to one another.

Submission

Ephesians 5:21, NIV

Submit to one another out of reverence for Christ.

Some struggle with the word *submit*, but I like the word because it is telling us to be supportive and courteous to one another. I believe your submission and love for the Lord will reflect in how well you submit and love your spouse.

Do you follow God's commands and love Him enough to make changes?

Are you living a life fully devoted to pleasing the Lord?

If you answer no to these questions, you may struggle in your marriage. God does not change, rather, He changes us. It is the same way in a marriage. You cannot change your spouse; you can only change yourself and your actions. Let God do the work in you before you commit to saying, "I do."

Take time to reflect on what type of wife you would like to be in your marriage?

_____
_____

Song: You Love Me Best by Elli Holcomb

He who loves his wife loves himself.

Day Five

Ephesians 5:28-29, NIV

In this same way, husbands ought to love their wives as their own bodies. He who loves his wife loves himself. After all, no one ever hated their own body, but they feed and care for their body, just as Christ does the church

How do you currently take care of your body both mentally and physically?

_____
_____
_____
_____
_____
_____

When you consider marrying someone, pay attention to how they treat and take care of themselves. This will reflect how well they will treat and care for you.

Song: Enough to Be Loved by Nia Purpose

Chapter Six

Note to leader: Begin each chapter by reflecting on what the group is thankful for. Ask if there are any prayer requests. These may be shared aloud or silently to pray.

What are you thankful for?

_____
_____
_____

Prayer requests

_____
_____
_____

Honor your father and mother

Day One

Do you know that every promise has a principle? Yes, many believe that everything good in the Bible applies directly to their lives. This is not to be confused with grace. God is a good Father who gives blessings to His children, but in the Bible, there are promises that align with right living. Think about a cause and effect: Every action in life has a reaction. God gives us promises that align with His principles. We see this at the start of Ephesians 6.

Ephesians 6:1-3, NIV

Children, obey your parents in the Lord, for this is right. "Honor your father and mother"—which is the first commandment with a promise— "so that it may go well with you and that you may enjoy long life on the earth."

How do you honor your mother and father? Is there anything you need to apologize or ask forgiveness for? If your parents are no longer alive, take time to pray and ask God to give you peace as you seek forgiveness. Forgiveness is for your wellbeing; it grows your ability to love and see people like God sees them.

_____
_____
_____
_____
_____
_____
_____

Song: Help Me to Walk by Nia Purpose

Work with enthusiasm, as though you were working for the Lord rather than for people.

Day Two

Ephesians:6:5-8,NLT

Slaves, obey your earthly masters with deep respect and fear. Serve them sincerely as you would serve Christ. Try to please them all the time, not just when they are watching you. As slaves of Christ, do the will of God with all your heart. Work with enthusiasm, as though you were working for the Lord rather than for people. Remember that the Lord will reward each one of us for the good we do, whether we are slaves or free.

Reflect: When you go to work or school who are you doing it for? Is it to impress other people, your parents, friends, or do you take pride in doing the right thing yourself?

_____
_____
_____
_____
_____
_____

Are there things that you do at work or school that you would not want anyone to see? Cutting corners, being late, gossiping, not giving your best? Let's be honest: We all struggle in some area because we are not perfect. However, when we reflect on our behaviors and remember everything we do should be done as unto the Lord, it helps change our behaviors and actions.

Take time to write a prayer asking the Lord to help you in any area you want to grow your character and work ethic.

_____
_____
_____
_____
_____
_____

Song: It's Working by William Murphy

Be strong in the Lord and in his mighty power.

Day Three

Ephesians 6:10, NIV

A final word: Be strong in the Lord and in his mighty power.

We have to remember that our strength comes from the Lord, not in our ability or our power. It is through God's power that anything is accomplished through us and with us.

I have learned, especially during COVID, that if something is stressing me out and I cannot do anything to fix or change it, it is out of my control. This means it belongs to the Lord, and I have to trust His will and way.

He is in control of everything.

He is in control of everything. We clearly do not have the authority to fix some situations, so we must lay it down at His feet. This is best expressed in **Matthew 28:11,** "Then Jesus said, 'Come to me, all of you who are weary and carry heavy burdens, and I will give you rest.'" We become overwhelmed and exhausted when we carry things we were never expected to carry. When things begin to get heavy, lay them down.

Pray and release.
What do you need to release to the Lord? What in your life feels heavy?

_____
_____
_____
_____
_____
_____
_____
_____
_____
_____

Song: Here Again by Elevation Worship

For we are
not fighting against
flesh-and-blood
enemies,
but against
evil rulers and
authorities of
the unseen world

Day Four

Ephesians 6:11-12, NIV

Put on all of God's armor so that you will be able to stand firm against all strategies of the devil. For we are not fighting against flesh-and-blood enemies, but against evil rulers and authorities of the unseen world, against mighty powers in this dark world, and against evil spirits in the heavenly places.

When we face trials and conflicts, we have to remember these verses in Ephesians 6. So many times, we start to believe we have problems with a certain person, but it is really a spirit within them that we are struggling with. It could also be a spirit that is within us as well. We must learn to pray and ask the Lord to remove these spirits from us and the ones we have strife with. Praying allows the Holy Spirit to move on our behalf and the enemy will flee.

Pray

When we see an evil spirit at work in a fellow brother or sister, pray earnestly for them instead of condemning them. Be spiritually mature and recognize there is a spiritual battle they are facing, and they may not even be aware they are in the middle of one.

Reflect on your behaviors and thoughts. Are you fighting against a spirit that is not from God? (bitterness, rage, anger, envy, despair)

_____
_____
_____
_____
_____
_____

We know the fruits of the Spirit are love, joy, peace, patience, kindness, goodness, faithfulness, gentleness, and self-control (Galatians 5:22, NLT). Ask the Holy Spirit to produce and cultivate the fruit of the Spirit in your daily life. Remember, before we can point out the transgressions of someone else, we must acknowledge and attend to our own. Read **Matthew 7:5 and Luke 6:42.**

Song: Fight for Me by GAWVI featuring Lecrae

Resist the enemy

Day Five

Ephesians 13:18, NLT

Therefore, put on every piece of God's armor so you will be able to resist the enemy in the time of evil. Then after the battle you will still be standing firm. Stand your ground, putting on the belt of truth and the body armor of God's righteousness. For shoes, put on the peace that comes from the Good News so that you will be fully prepared. In addition to all of these, hold up the shield of faith to stop the fiery arrows of the devil. Put on salvation as your helmet, and take the sword of the Spirit, which is the word of God. Pray in the Spirit at all times and on every occasion. Stay alert and be persistent in your prayers for all believers everywhere.

Pray in the Spirit at all times and on every occasion.

I encourage you to watch the video messages by Dr. Tony Evans who explains the full armor of God so well. Dr. Evans has also written a book titled, "Prayers for Victory in Spiritual Warfare." This book consists of specific prayers to pray over different areas of life, covering each piece of the armor of God. The book is powerful and so are the prayers. I can attest that the prayers are heard by God, and I have experienced peace, deliverance, and breakthrough in many areas.

Stay Alert

Ephesians 6:23-24, NIV

Peace be with you, dear brothers and sisters, and may God the Father and the Lord Jesus Christ give you love with faithfulness. May God's grace be eternally upon all who love our Lord Jesus Christ.

I love how Paul ends this letter. It is so peaceful and reassuring that every day, no matter what we face or experience, everything in life will be okay. God, our Father, cares for us. The enemy does not win, and this world does not win. God wins and with Him, we win too! Stand strong in the Lord and live with thankfulness and joy because God loves you more than you will ever comprehend.

Song: Never Lost by Elevation Worship

Everything in life will be okay.

God wins and with Him, we win too!

Leaders Guide

If you are leading this Bible study, glory to God! Coming together with others to share and dive deeper into the Word allows for the Holy Spirit to move and speak through you to others. I personally enjoy reading and speaking about the Word of God above anything else in the world. Over time, I pray this will become a great joy for you too, if it is not already. I used to have no desire or motivation to read the Word, but then I was introduced to the Bible app and videos through the Bible Project. The words and stories started to click and make sense to me. I was able to relate to what I was reading and began to apply the scriptures to my life. As you read you will want to know more and share more. It truly is a gift from our Lord.

Begin by welcoming your guests

Maybe your guests have been to 50 Bible studies, or perhaps this is their first one. In either case, lead it like it is the last one you will ever get to lead. God has placed it on your heart to lead and guide others through His word and trust me when I say, He is well pleased with you and will guide your conversations.

Next, lead with thanksgiving

Depending on the days you meet, one way to get the ladies

comfortable is by starting with sharing some of the things for which you are thankful. Tuesdays and Thursdays pair well with this exercise. As the leader, you may have to start first. This sets the tone for an environment of gratitude and allows for your heart and the hearts of the group members to soften and reflect on just how many blessings the Lord has provided. Big and small things such as eyesight, food, shelter, families, careers, and cars, among a host of other things are all fair game. Do this every time you gather together. Paul is huge on giving thanks to the Lord and we should desire to follow the model he set for us.

Question to pose

One question to begin every study would be: What do you hope to gain from this study? Have the ladies write their responses on notecards and you can allow them to keep it, or you can keep them in an envelope. These will be reviewed at the end of the study.

Open with prayer

Remember this time together is strictly devoted to our Great and Majestic Father. He will lead the conversations and He can provide questions and revelations not provided in this study. Follow His lead.

www.ingramcontent.com/pod-product-compliance
Lightning Source LLC
Chambersburg PA
CBHW072037110526
44592CB00012B/1449